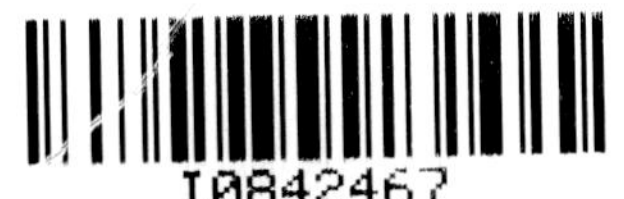

Beautiful Birds

An Adult Coloring Book

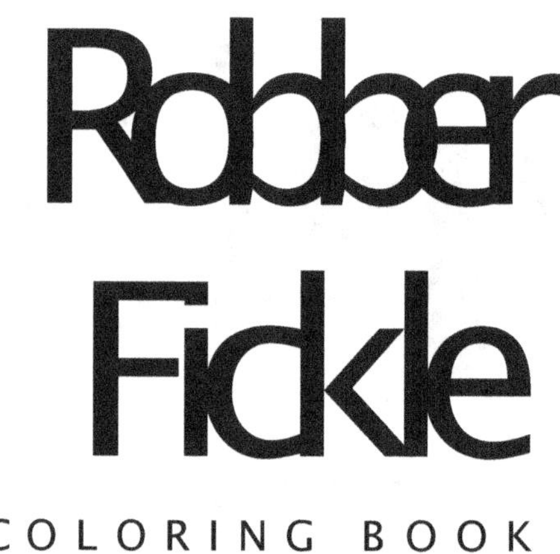

For Any Question and Suggestions
robberfickle@gmail.com

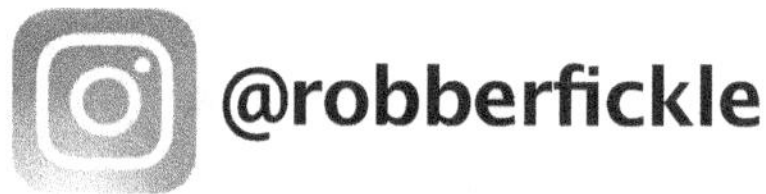

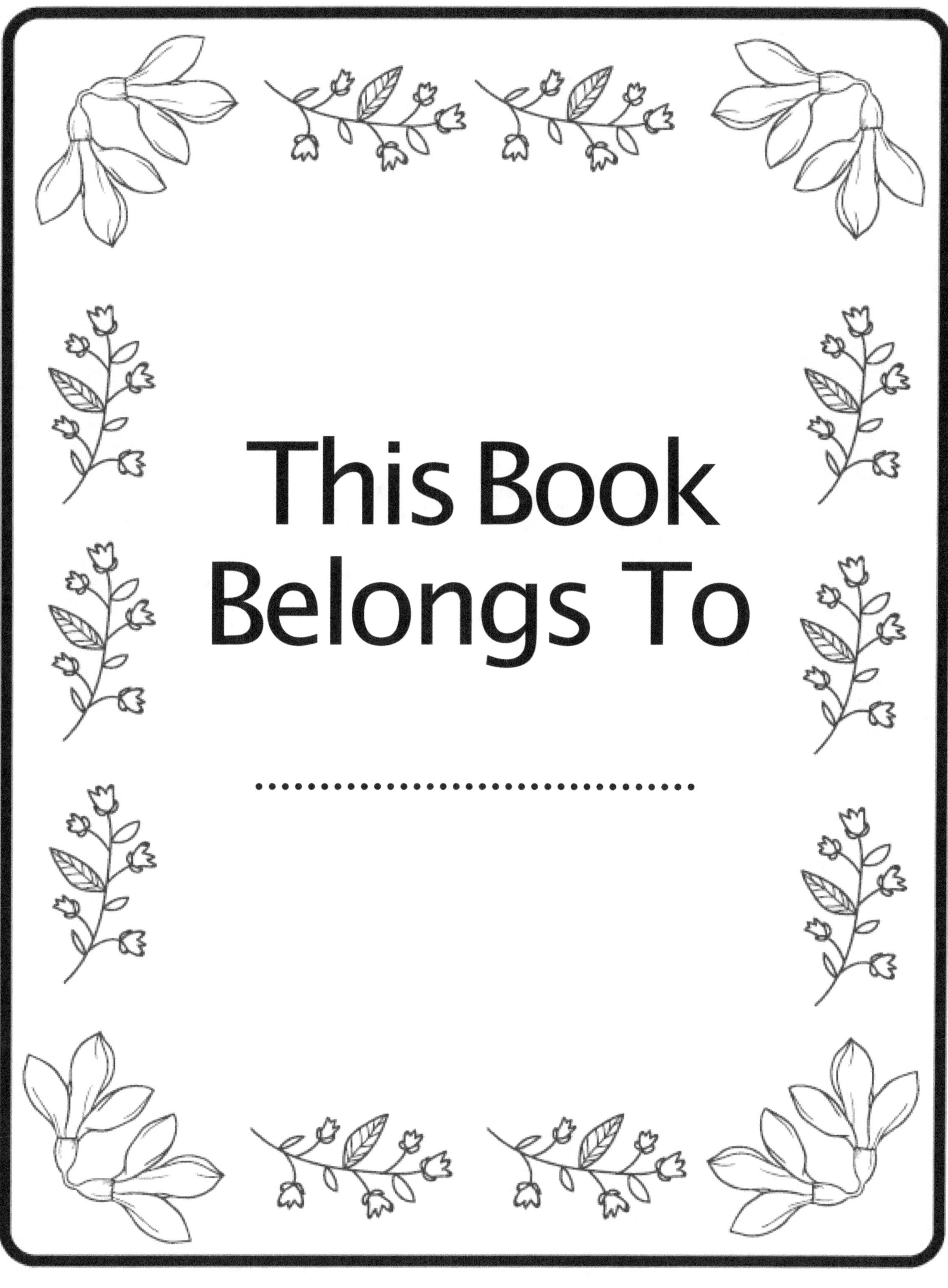
This Book
Belongs To
....

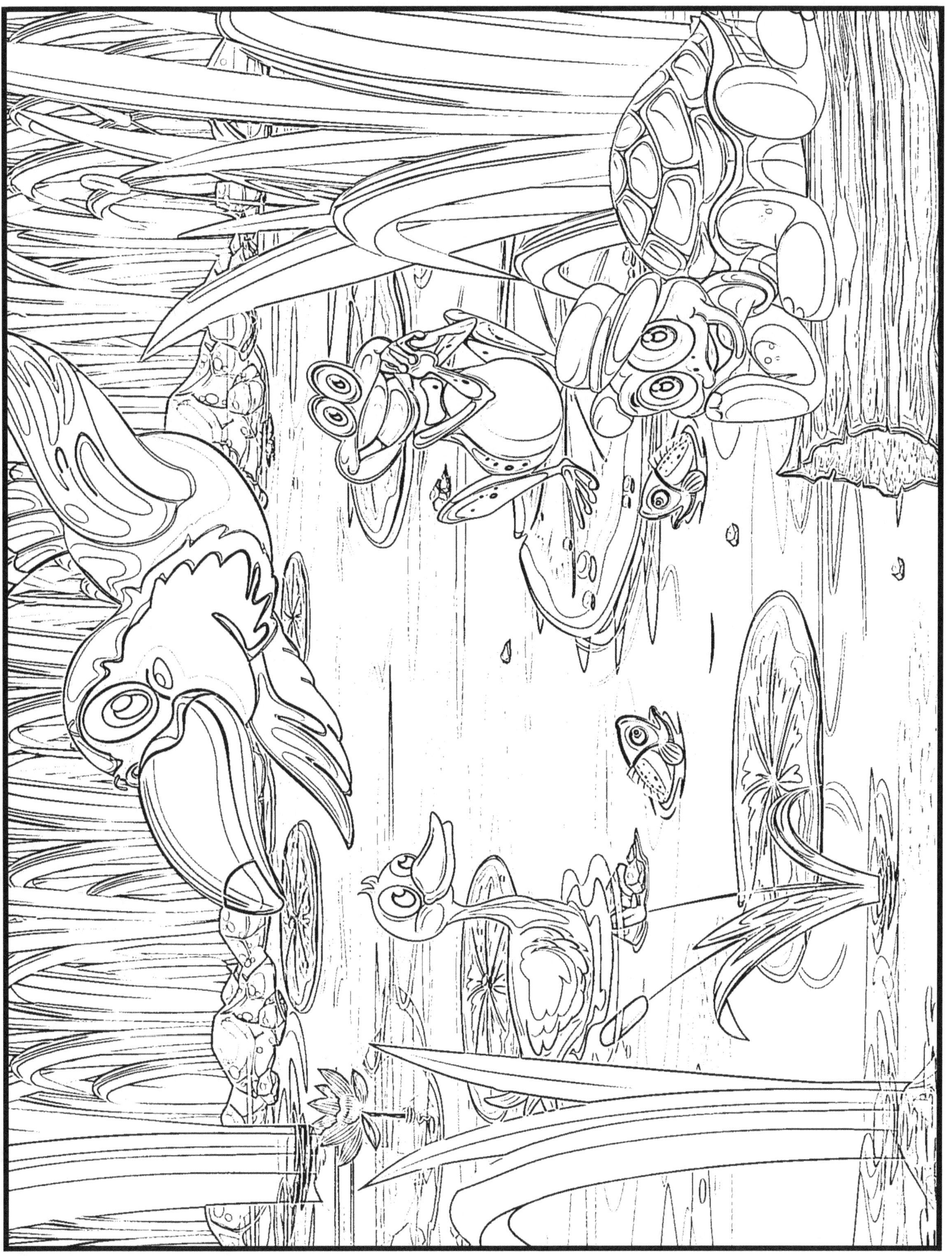

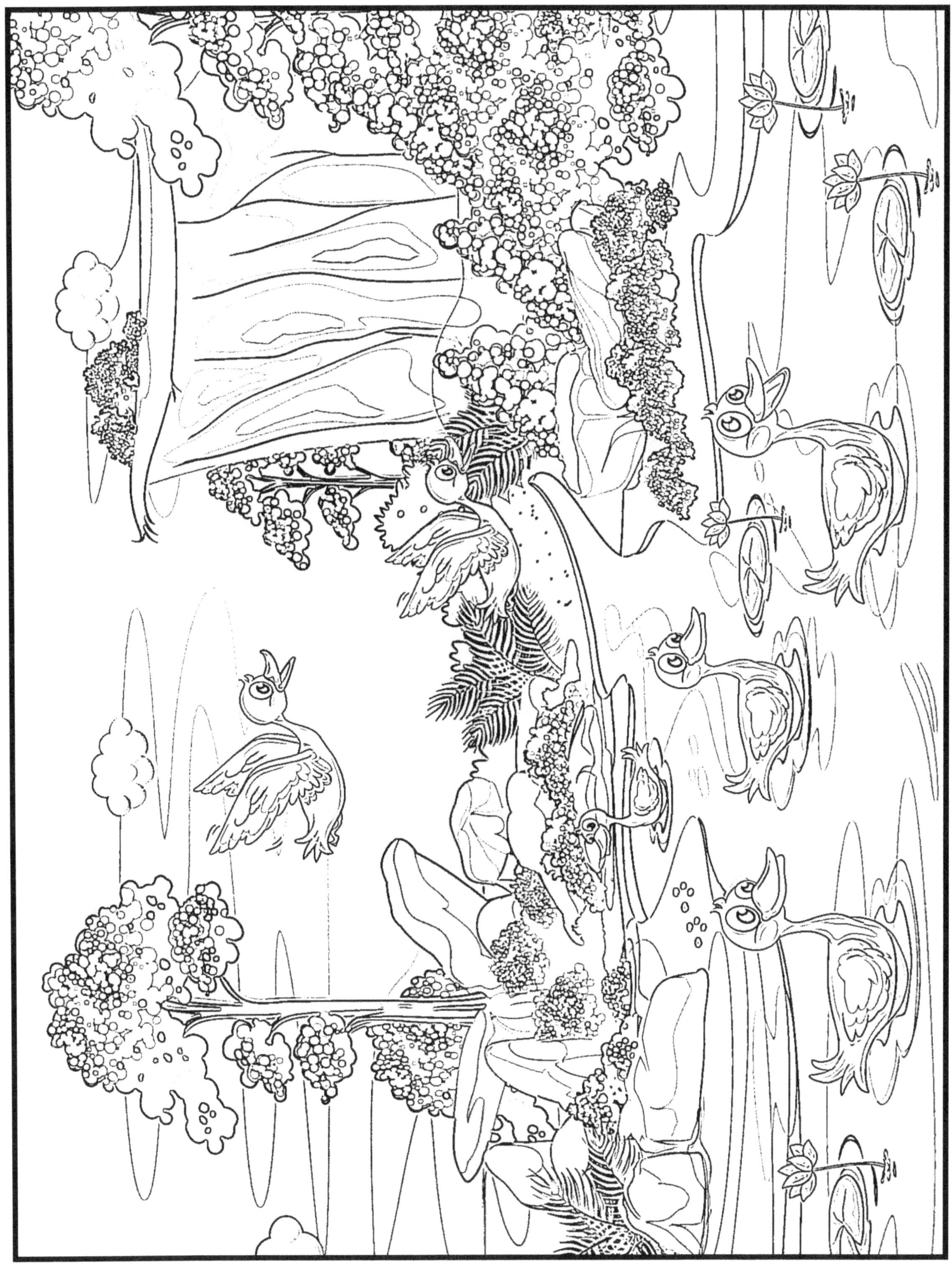

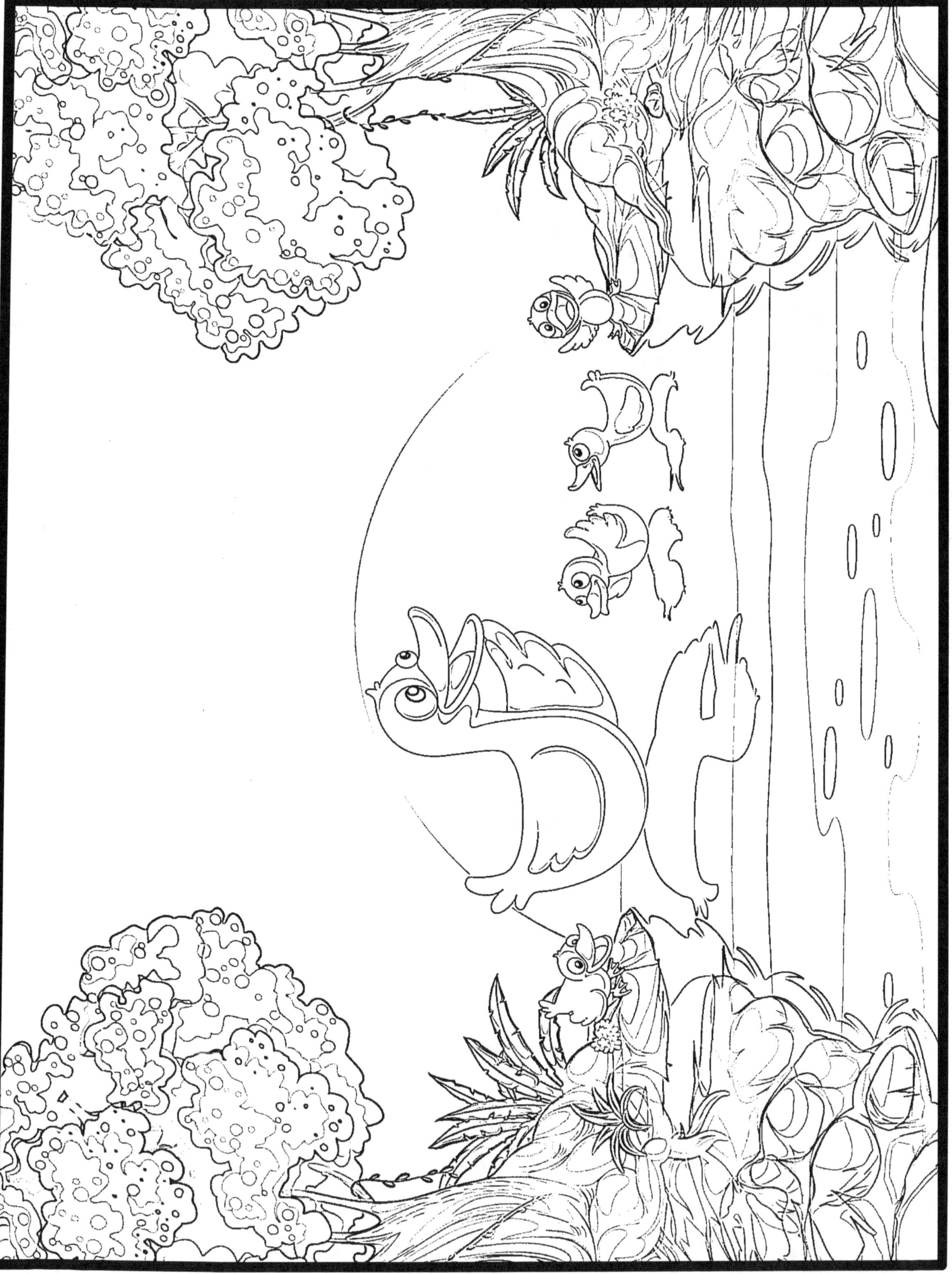

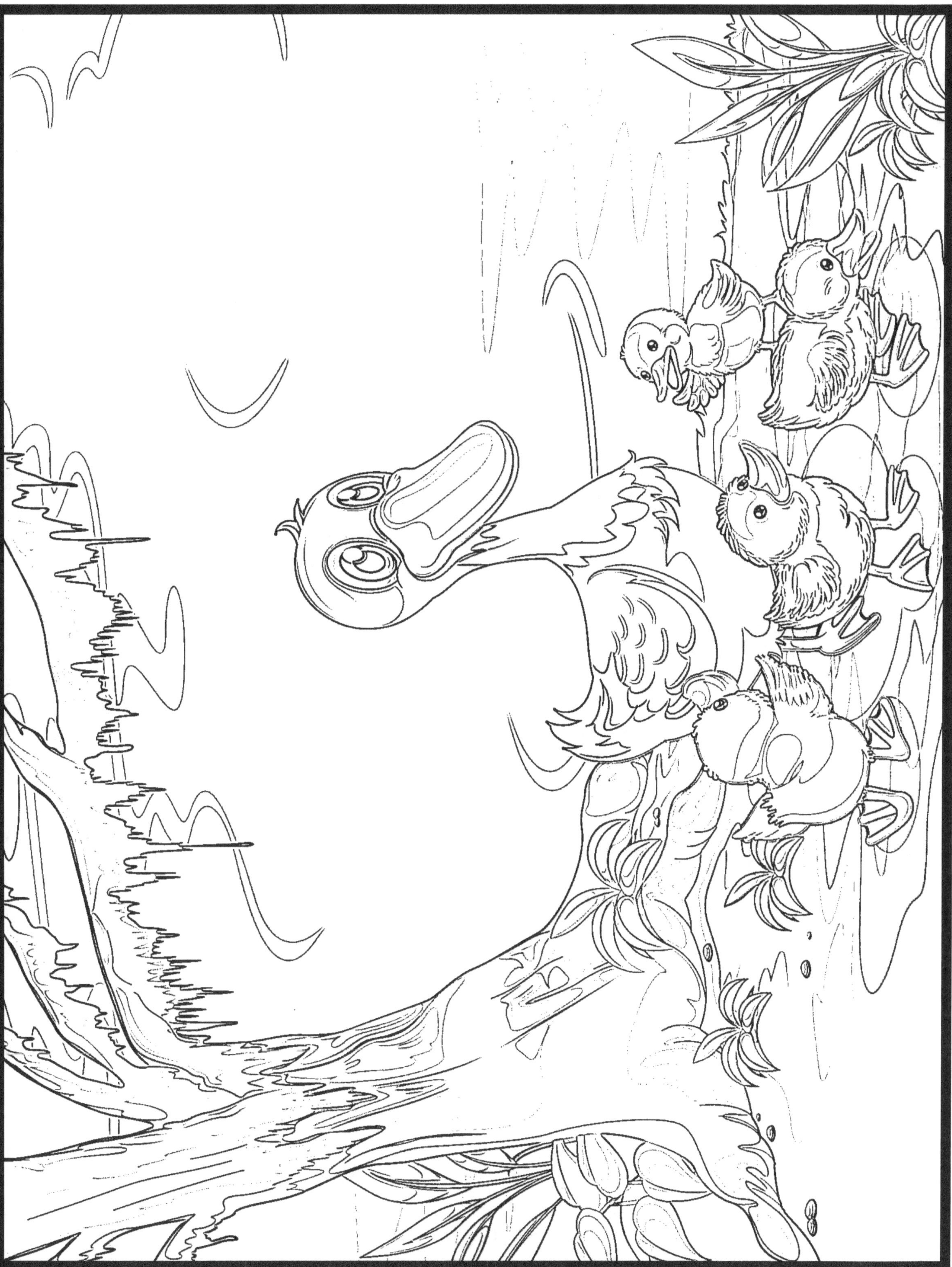

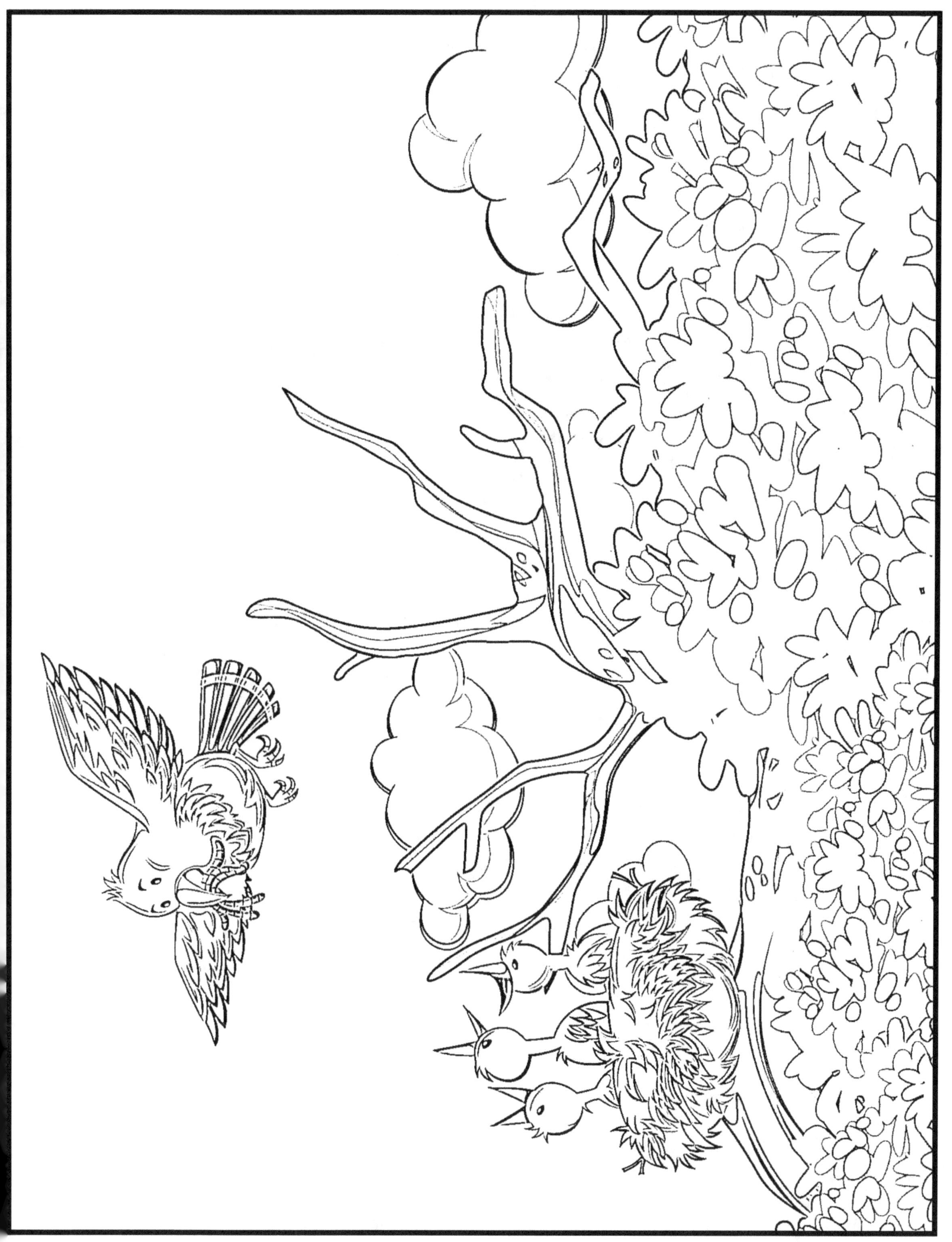

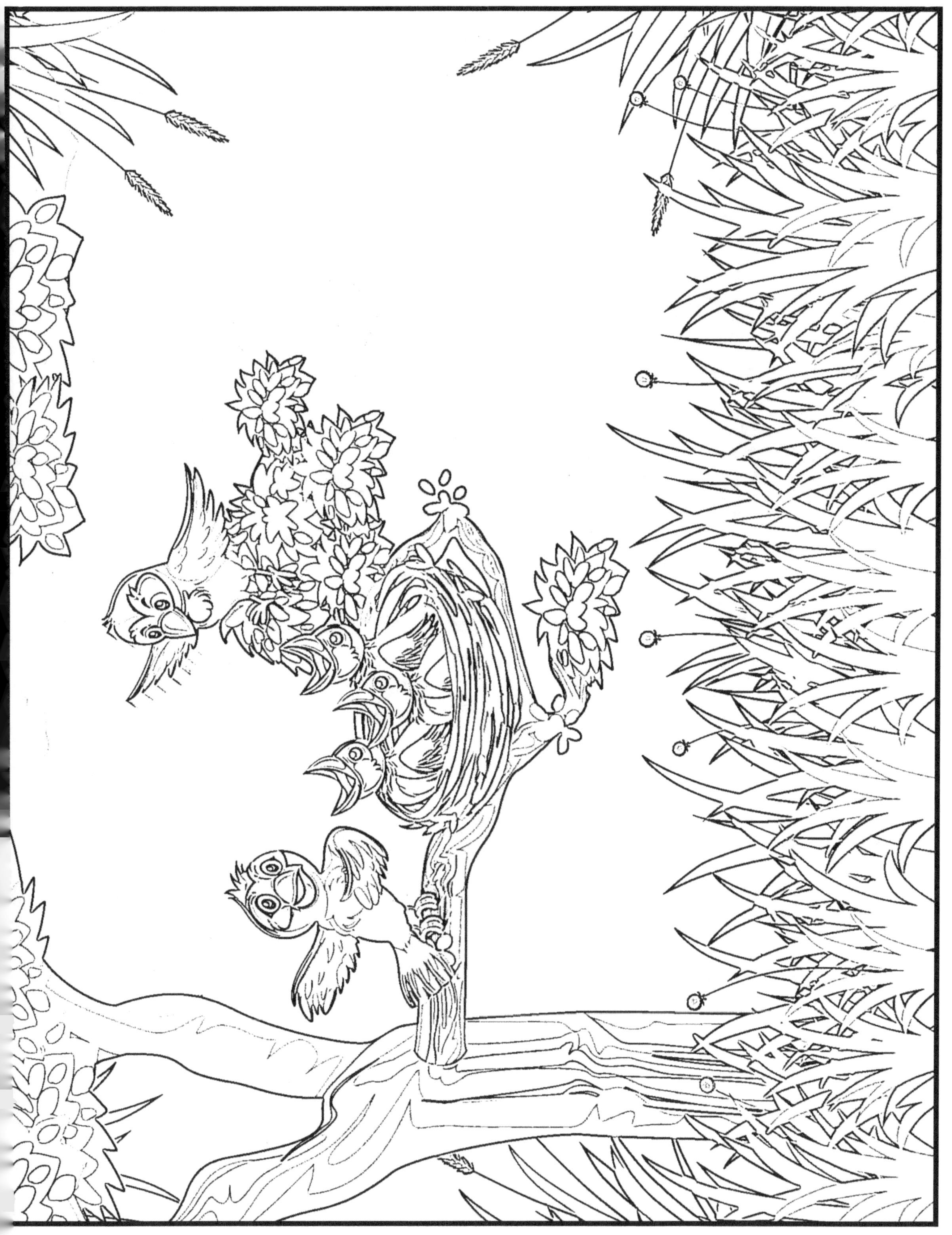

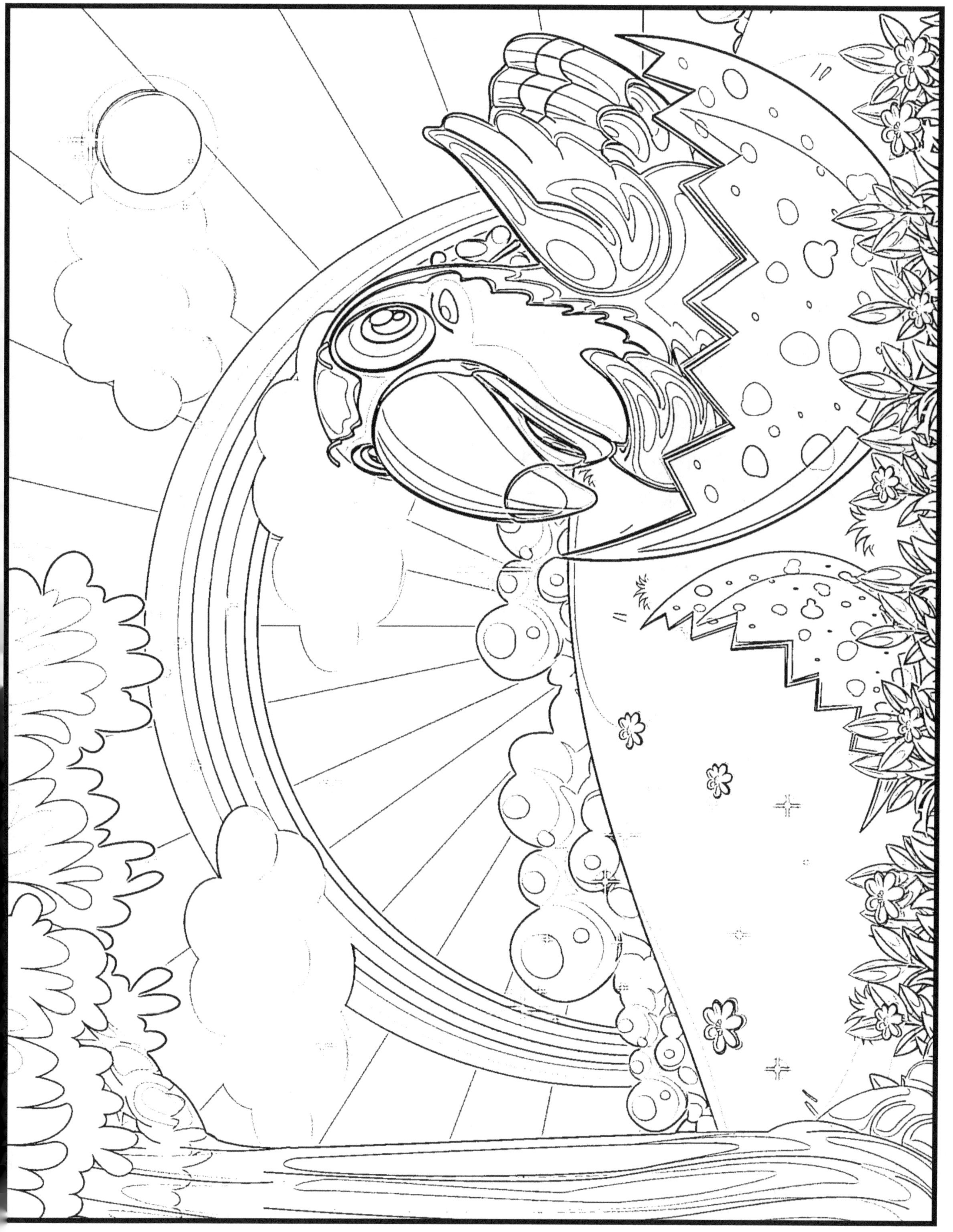

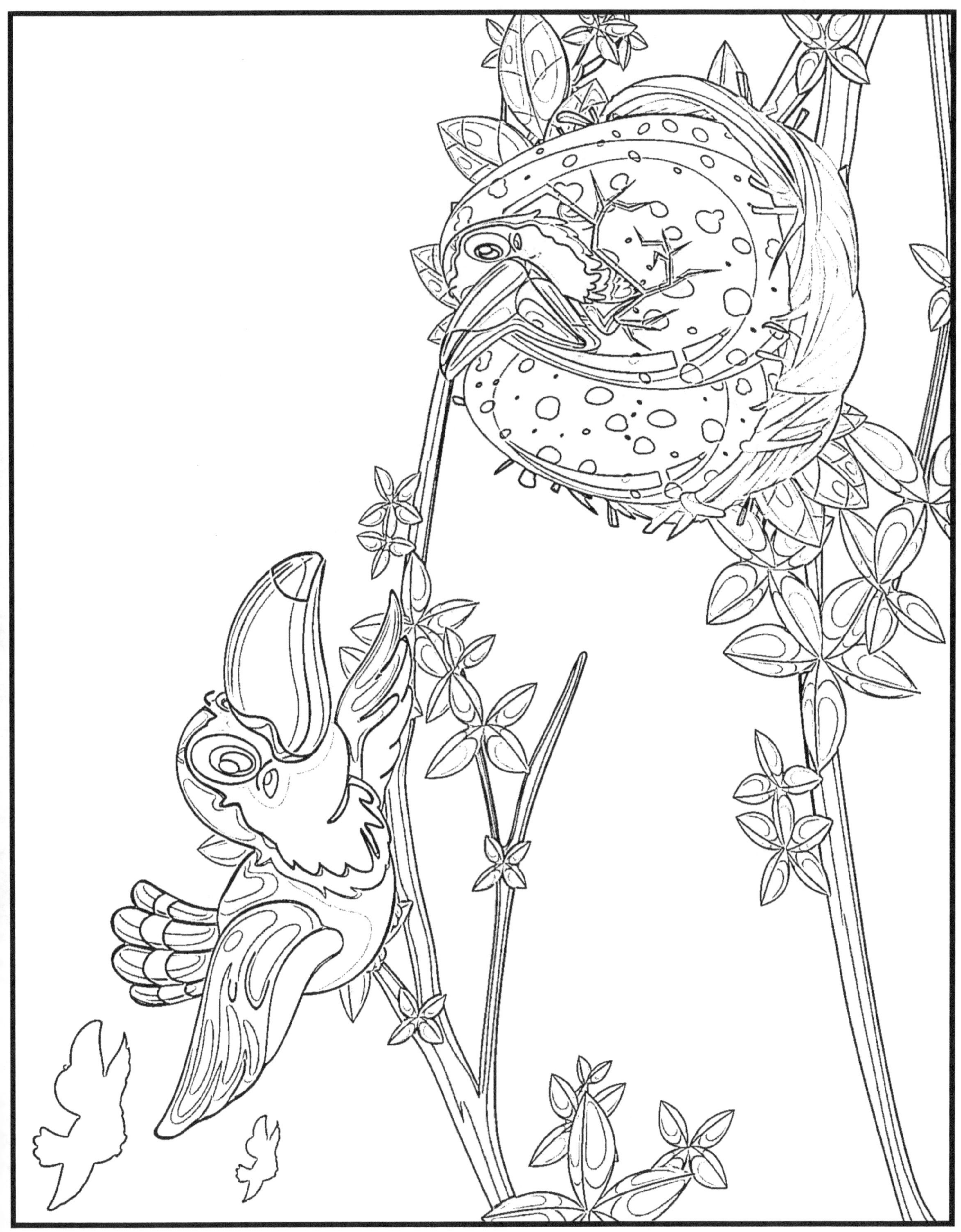

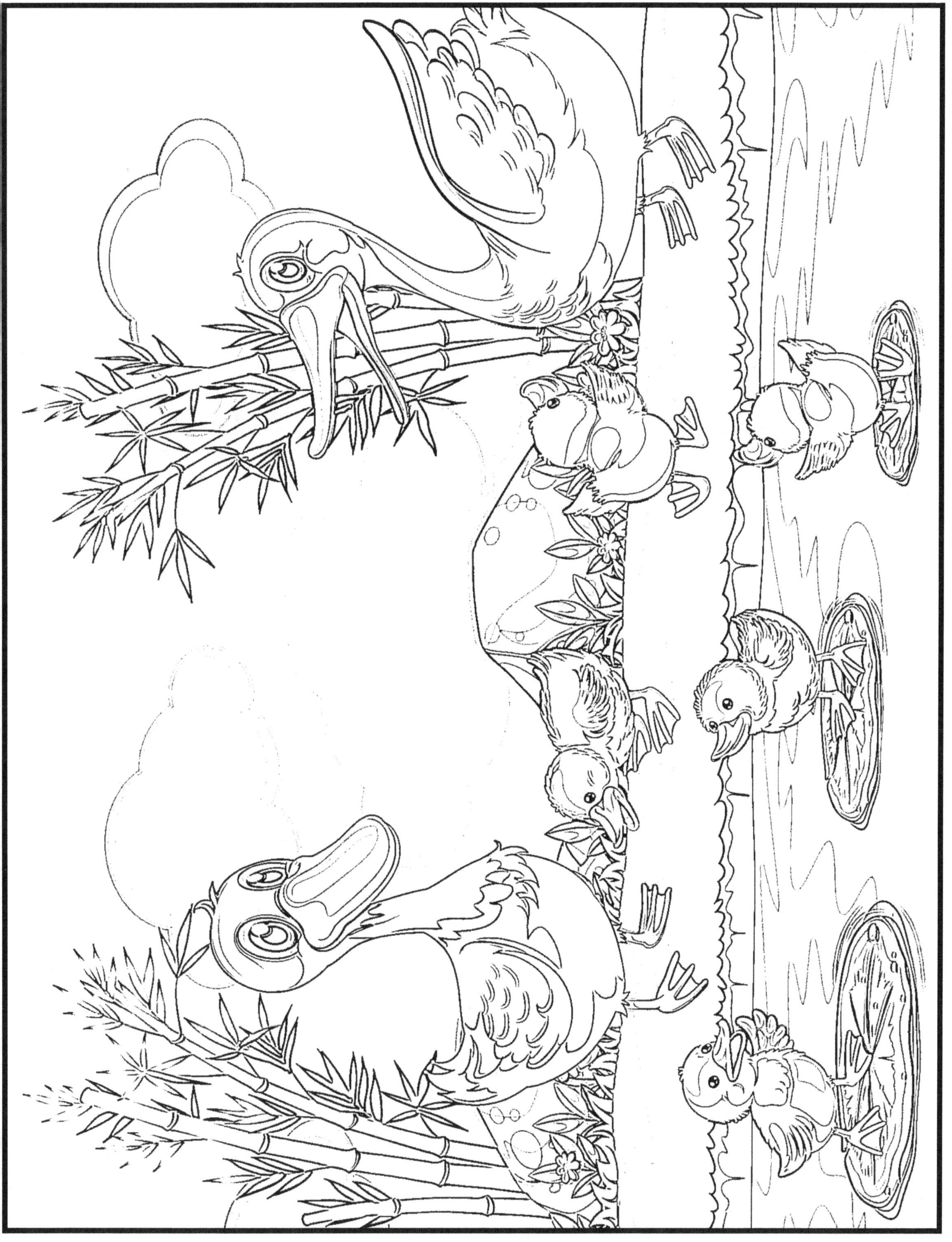

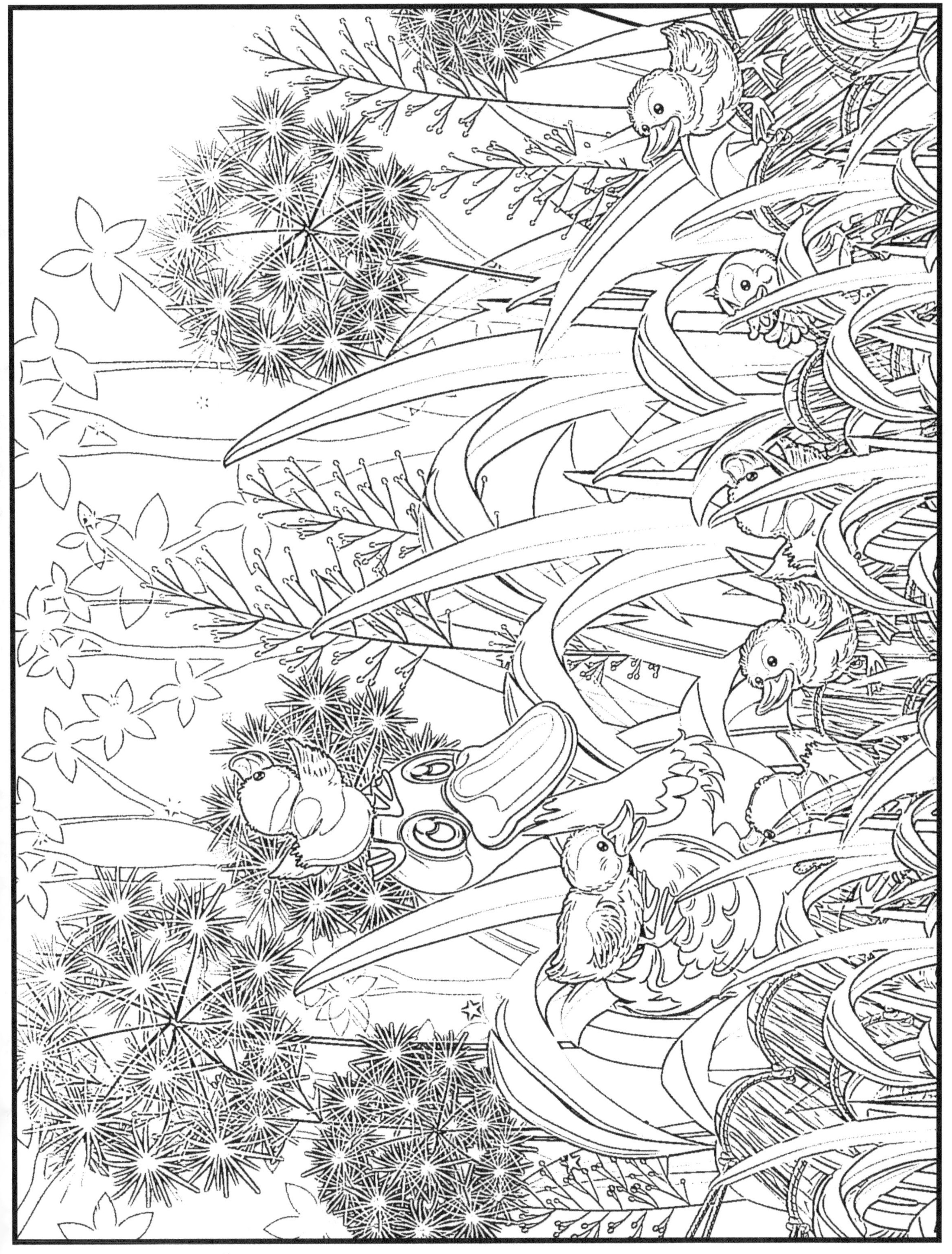

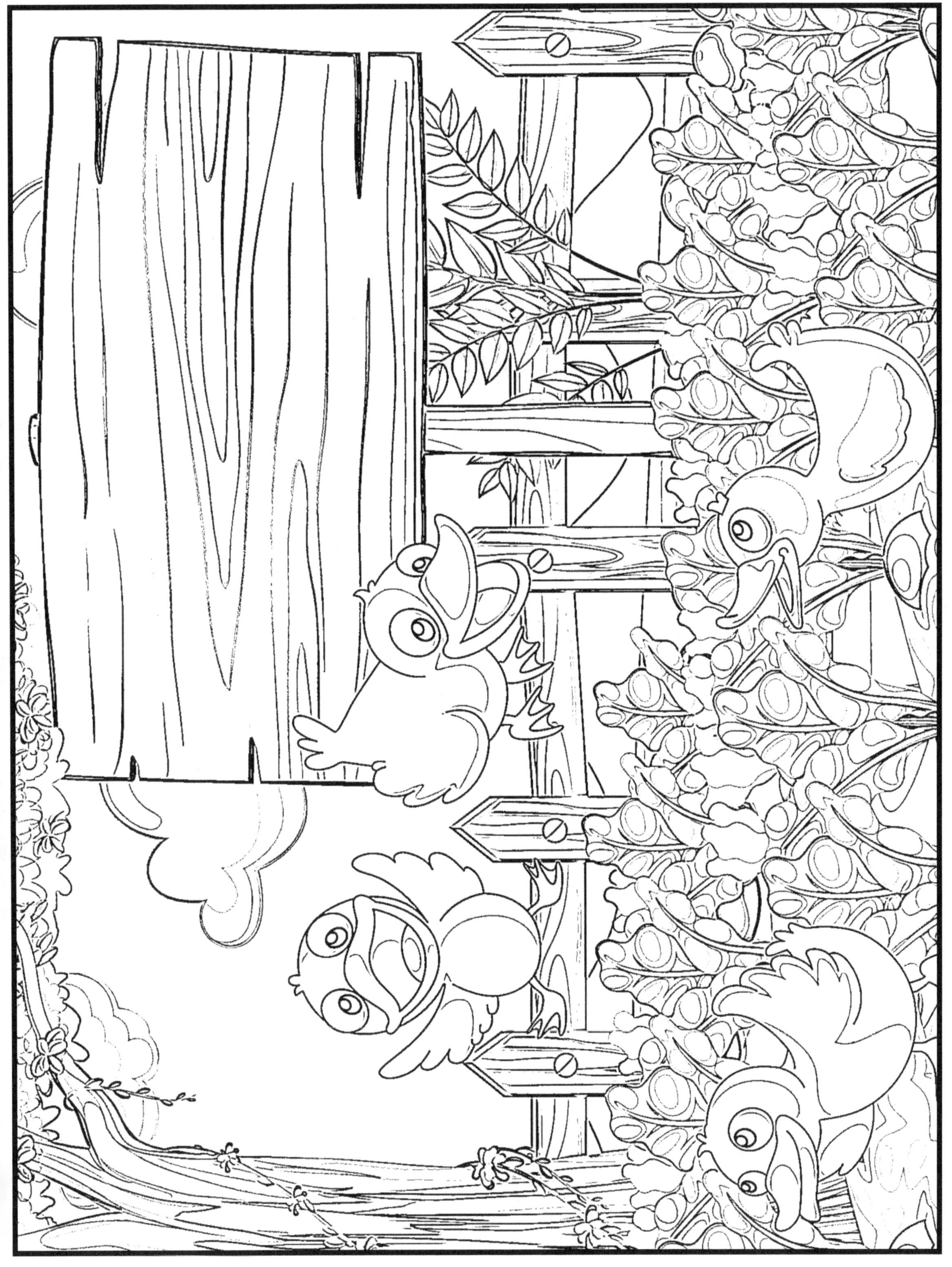

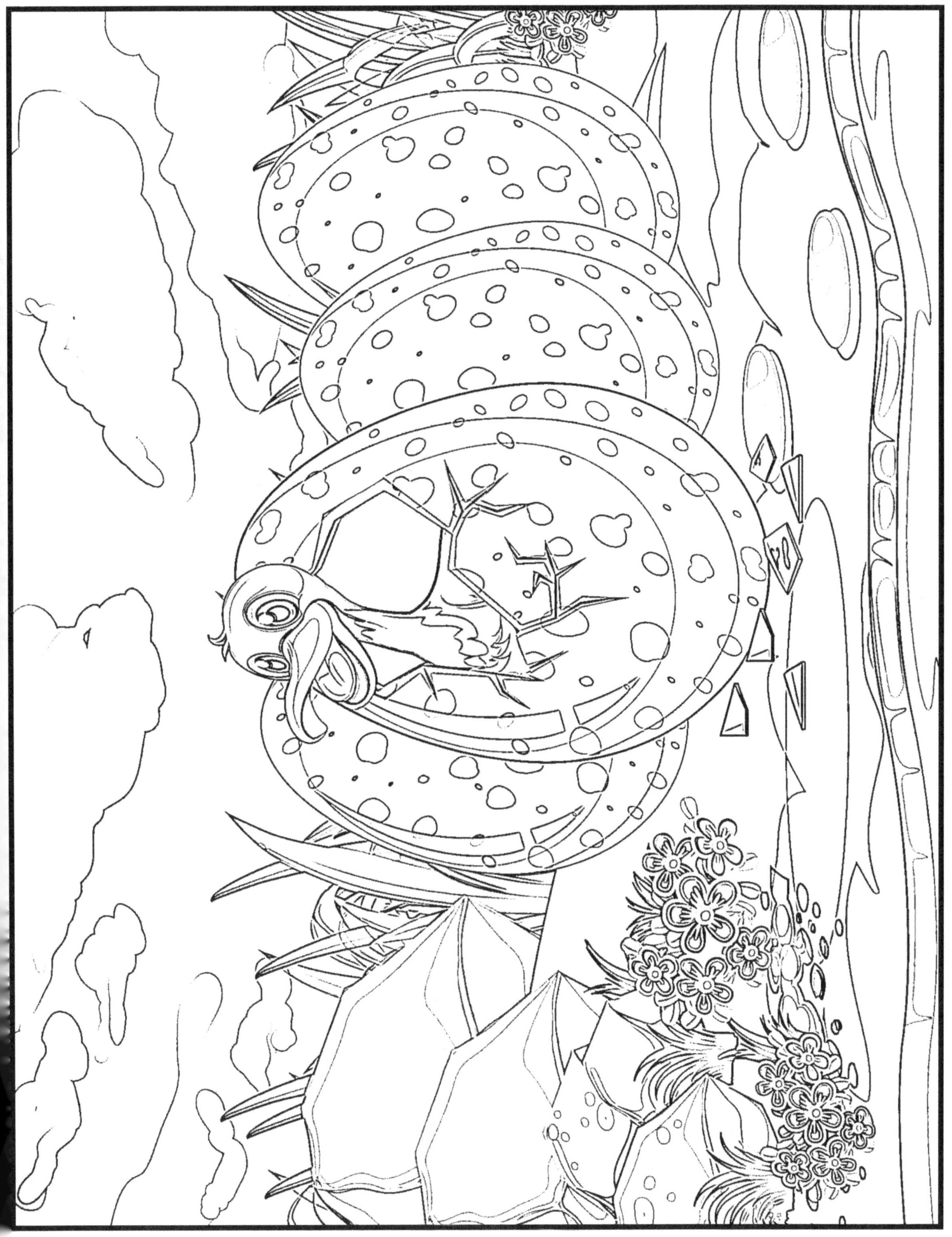

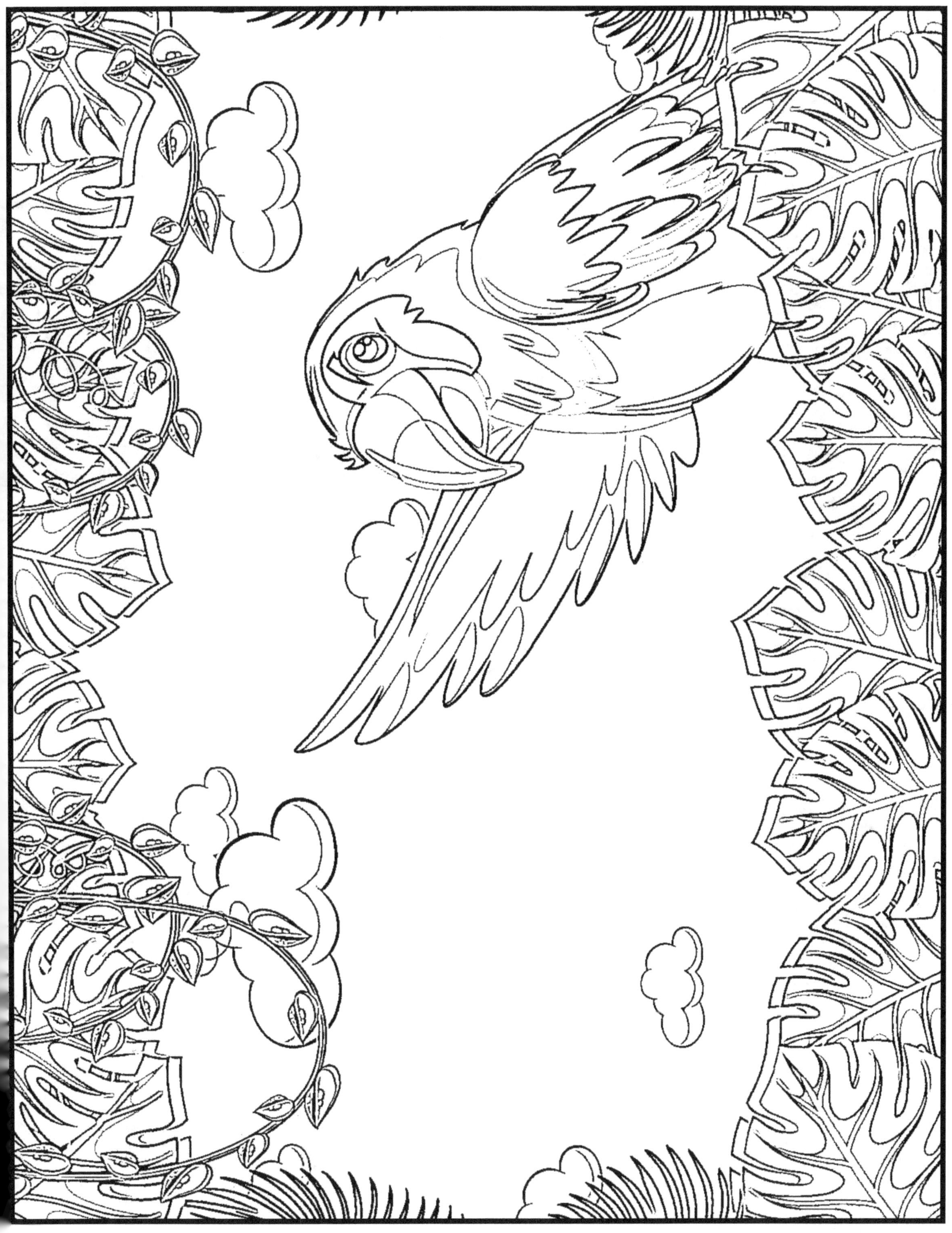

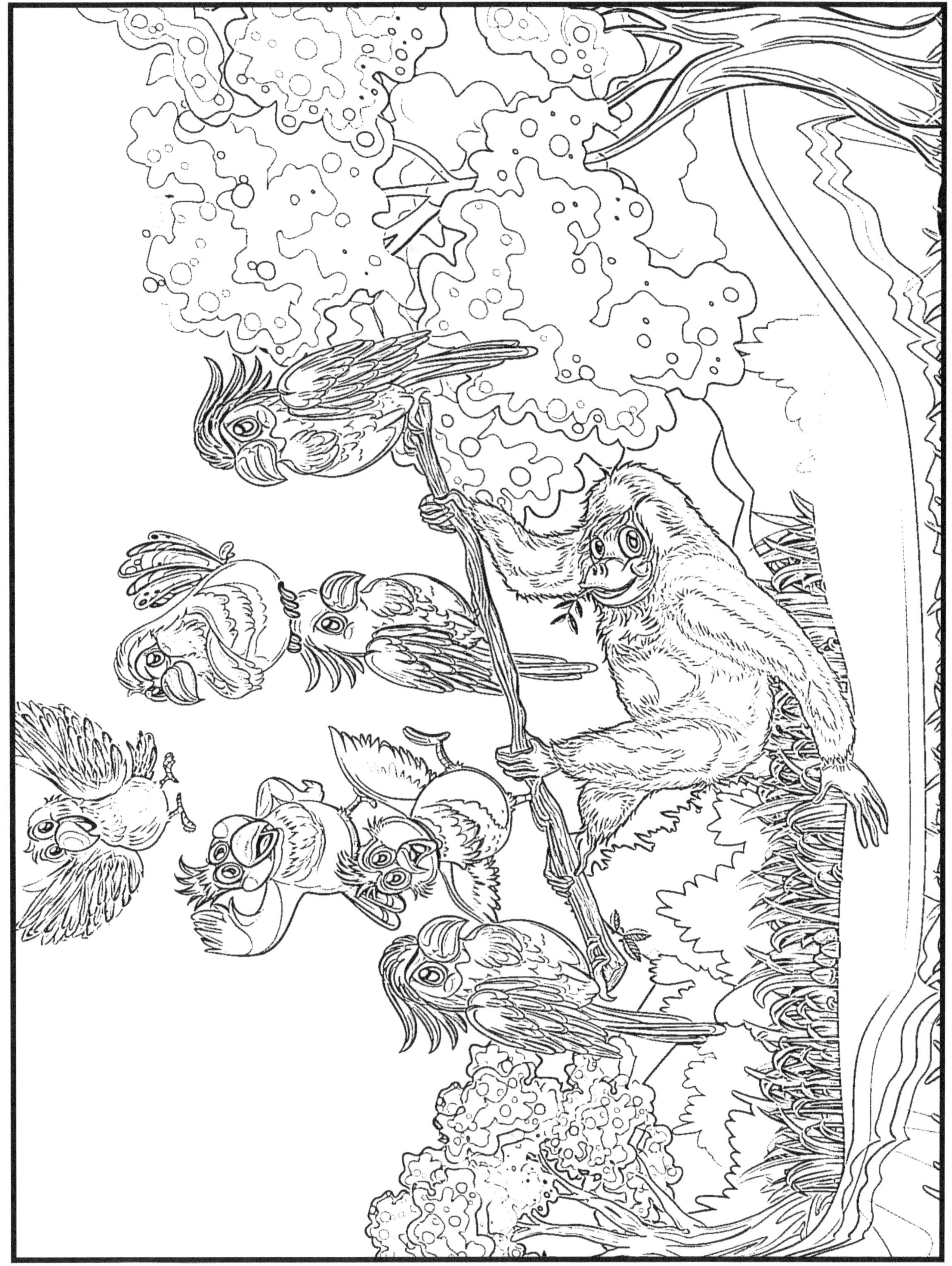

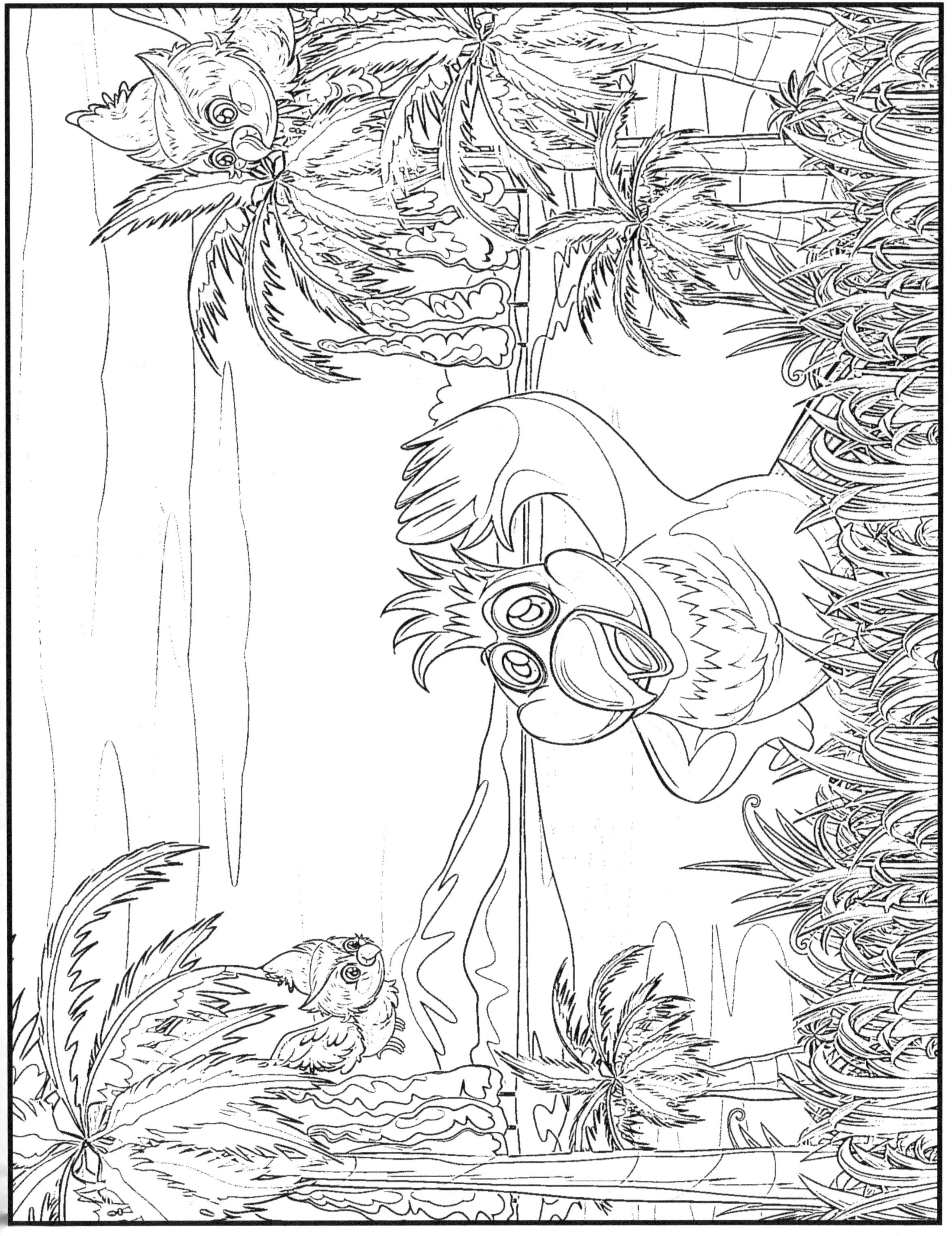

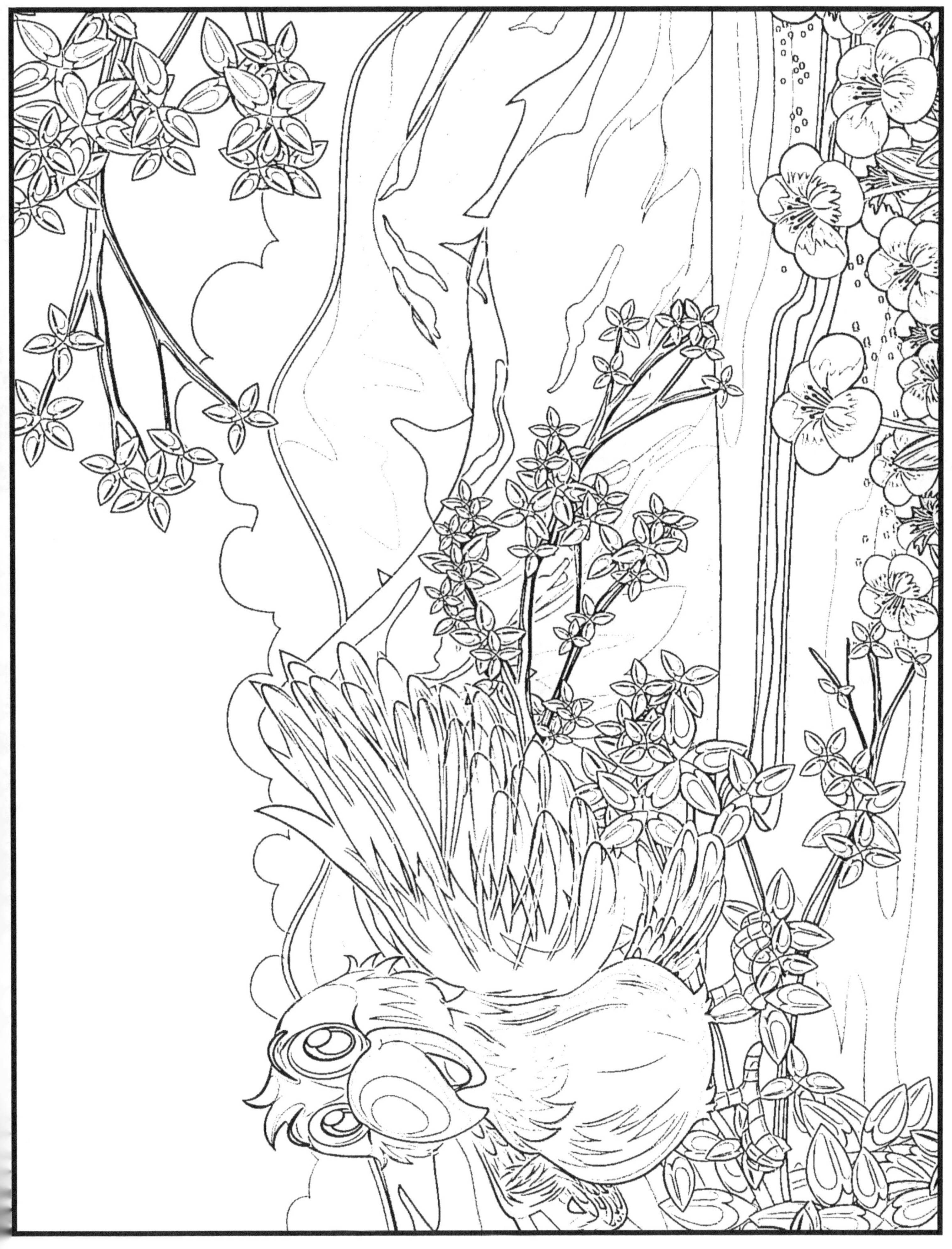

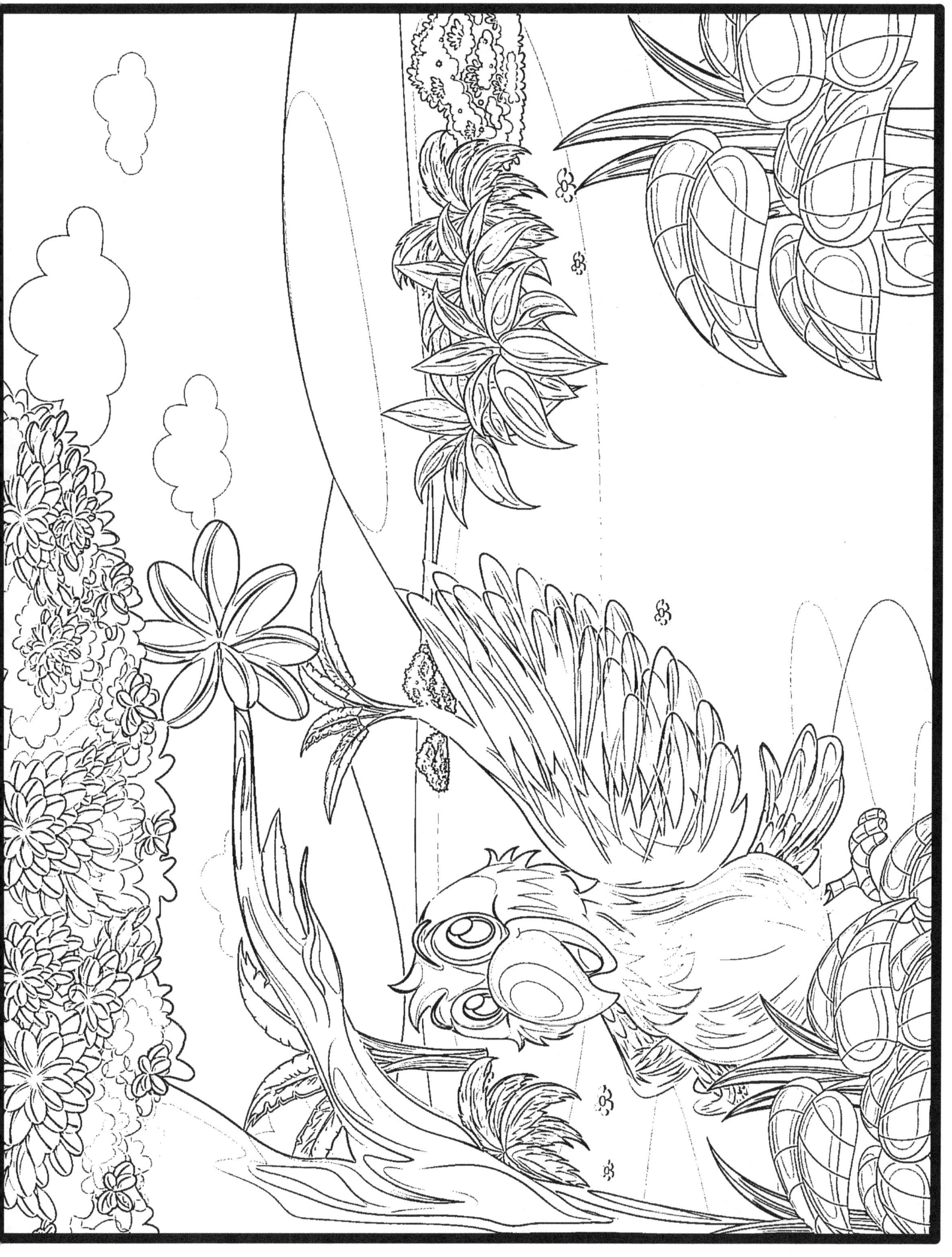

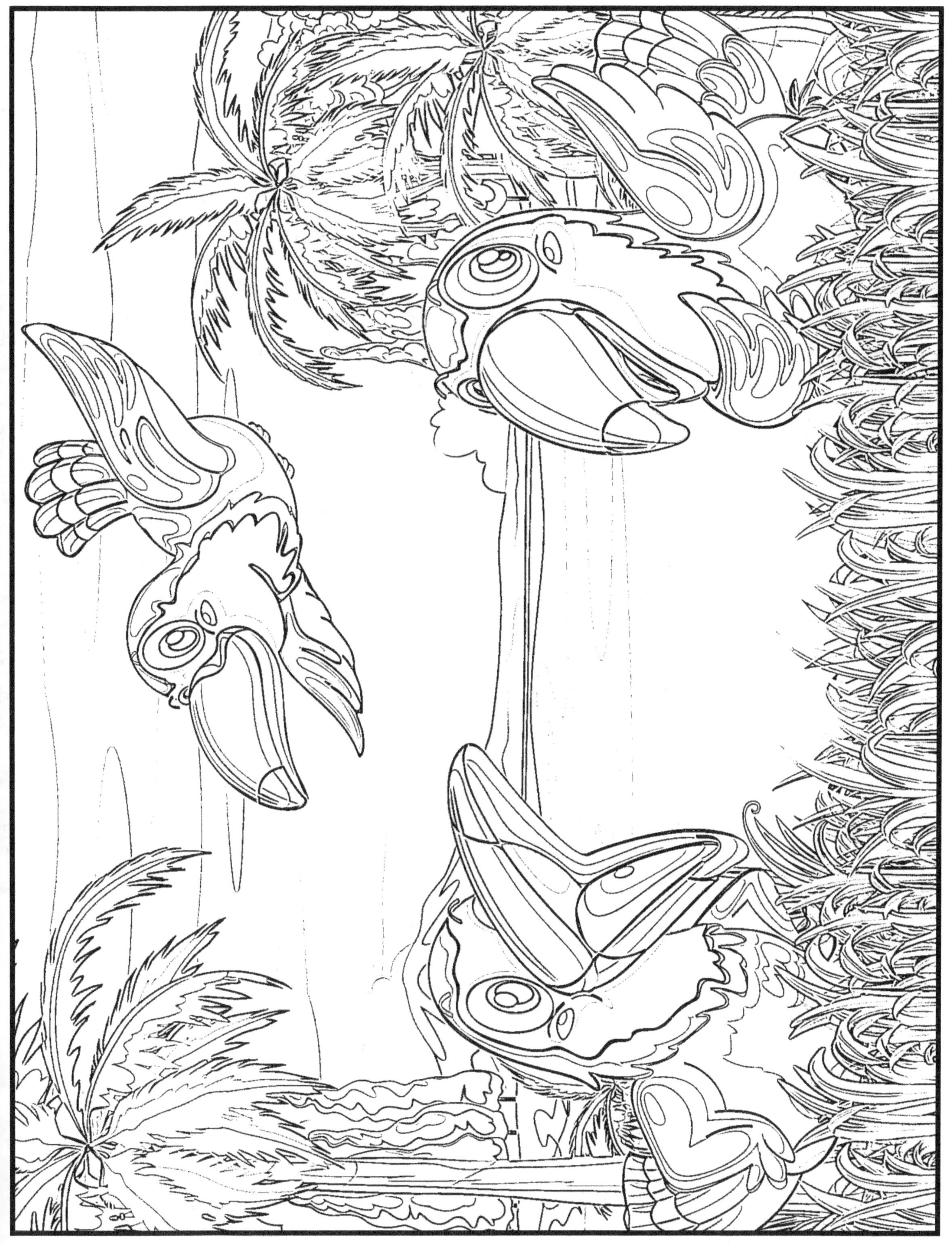

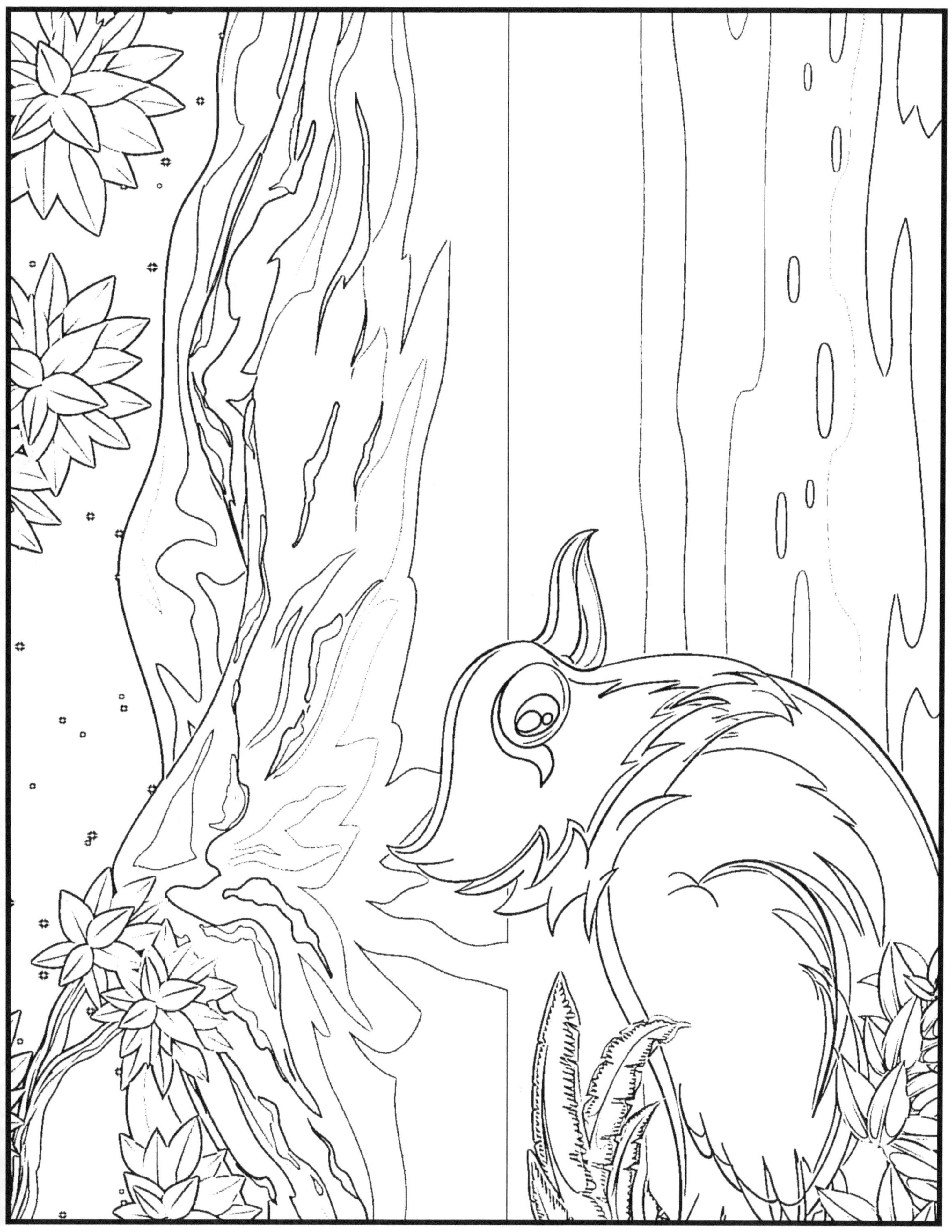

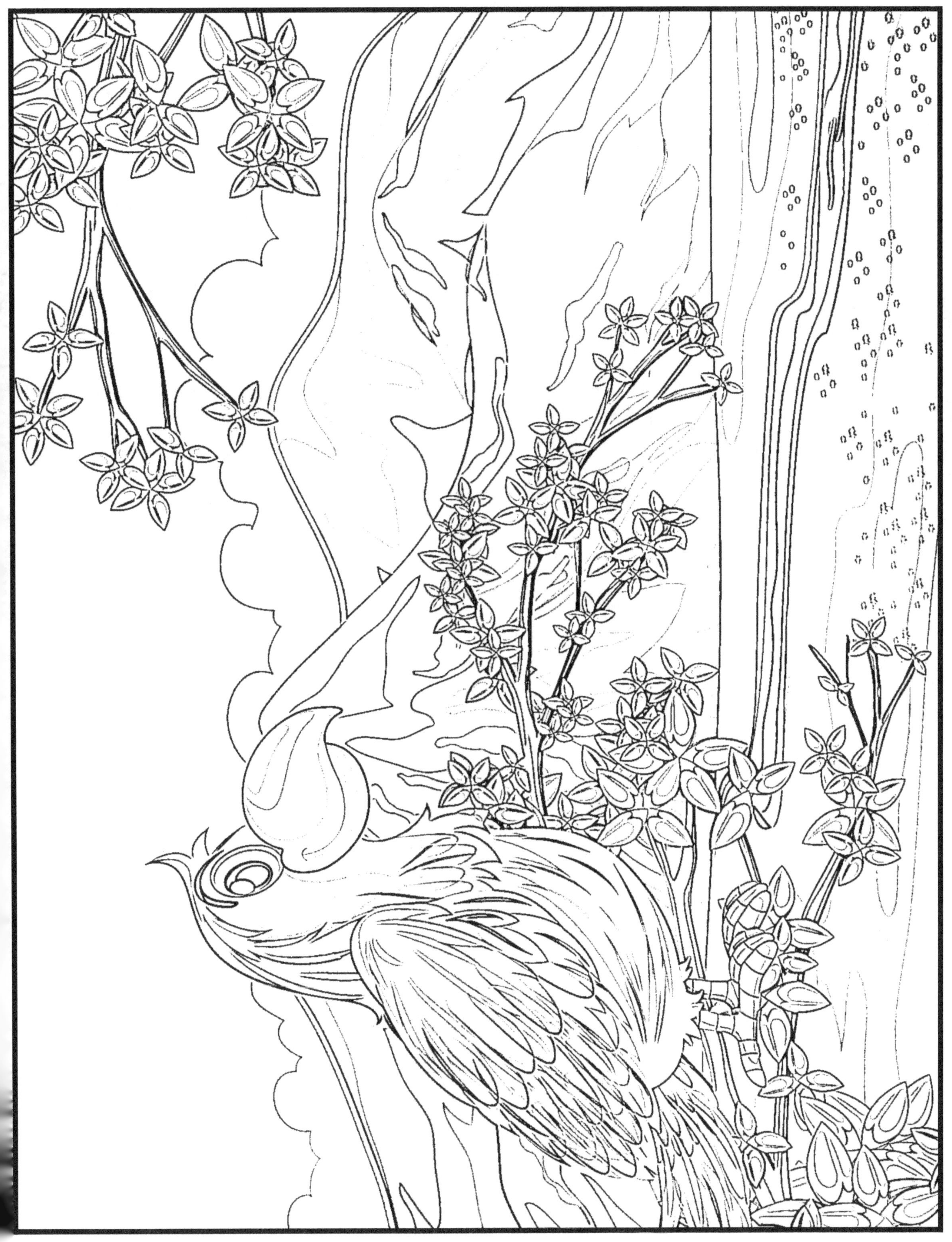

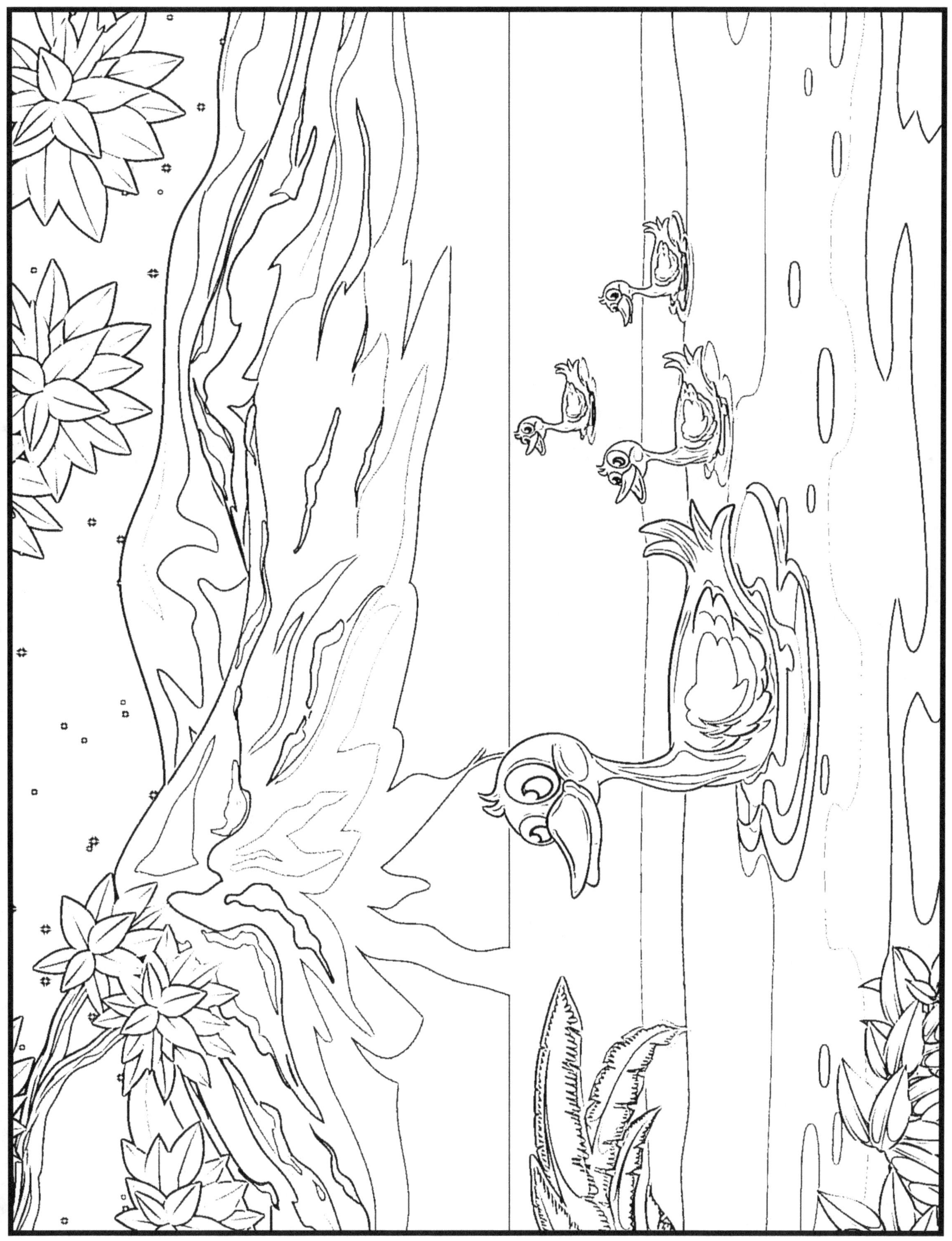

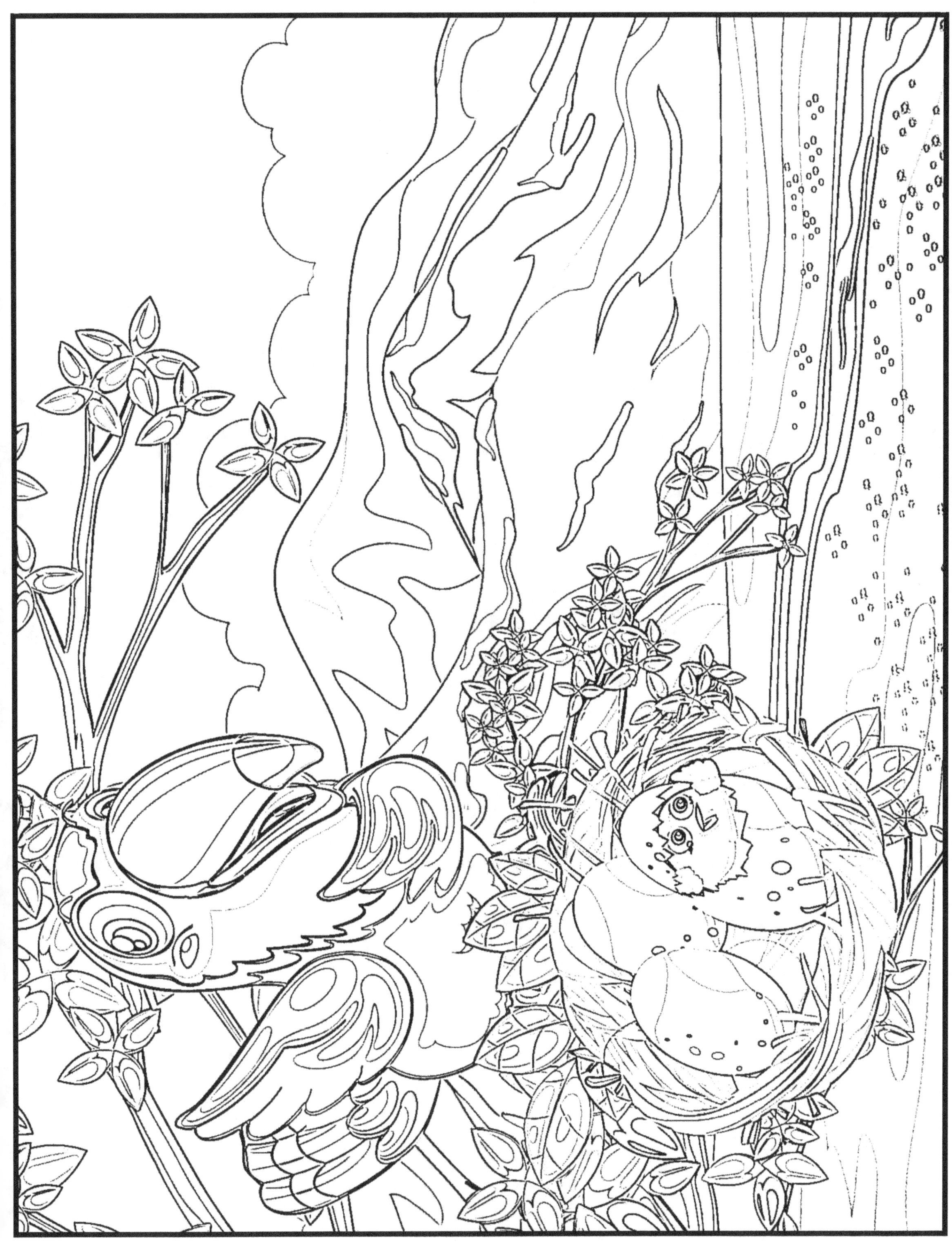

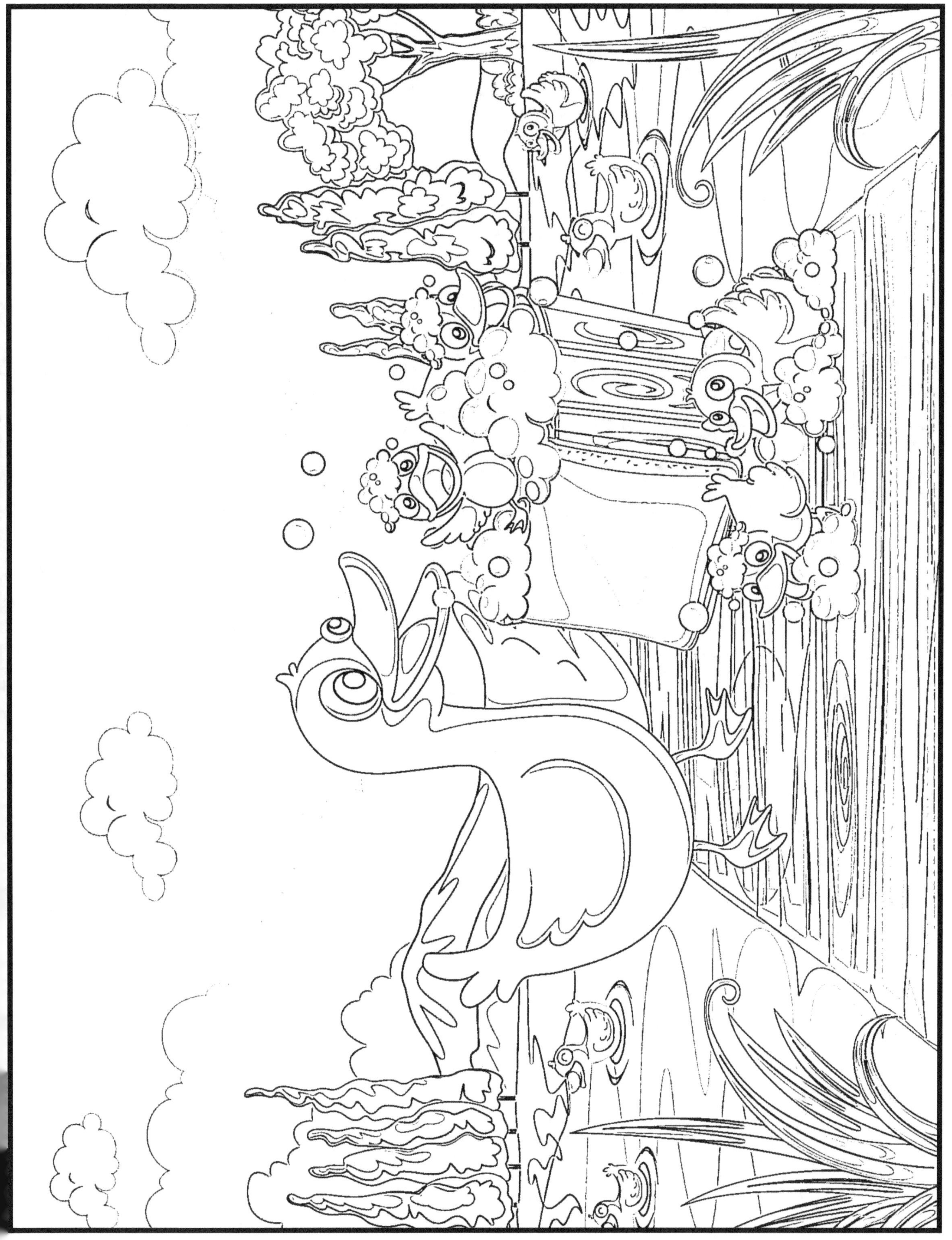

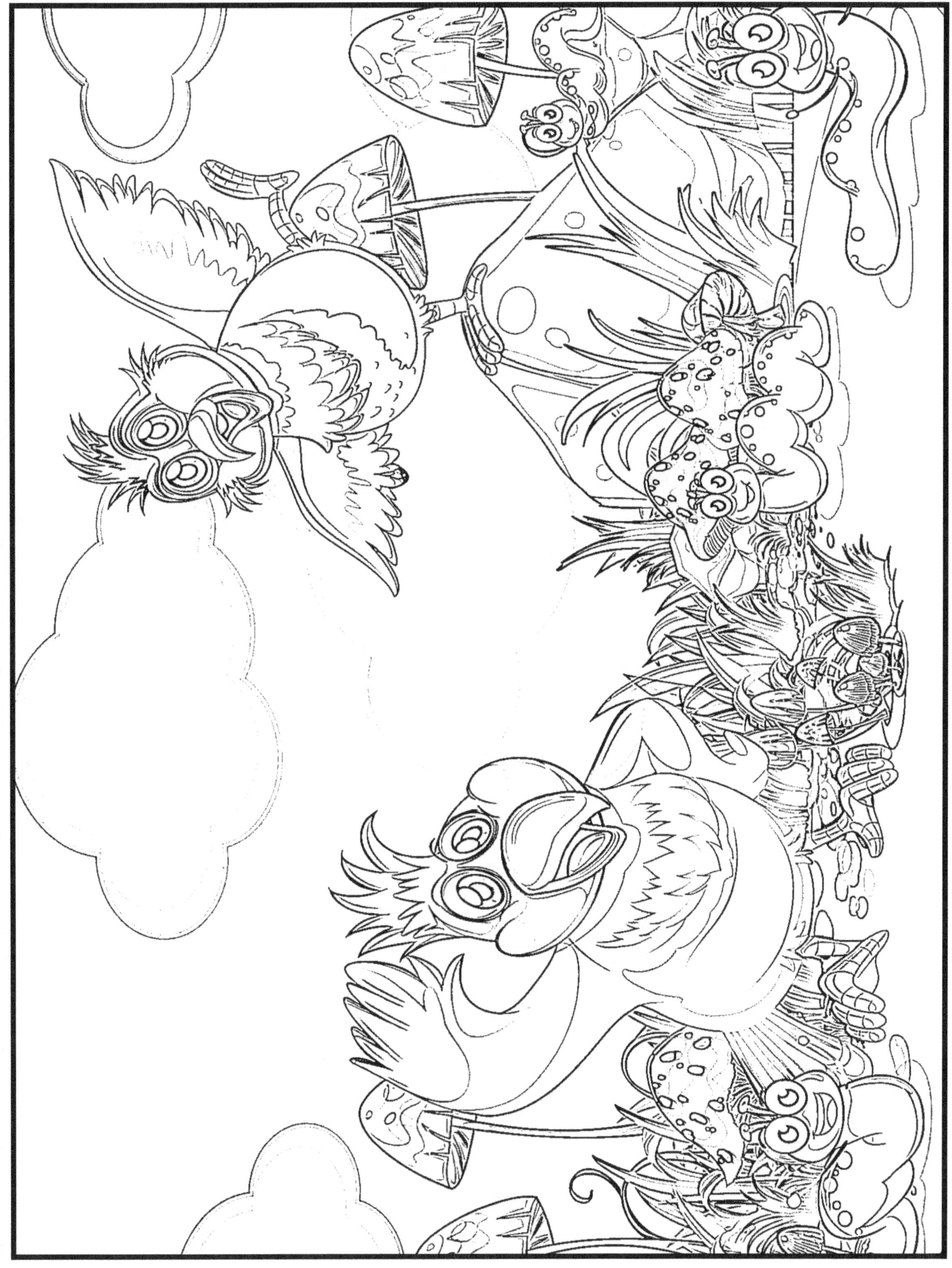

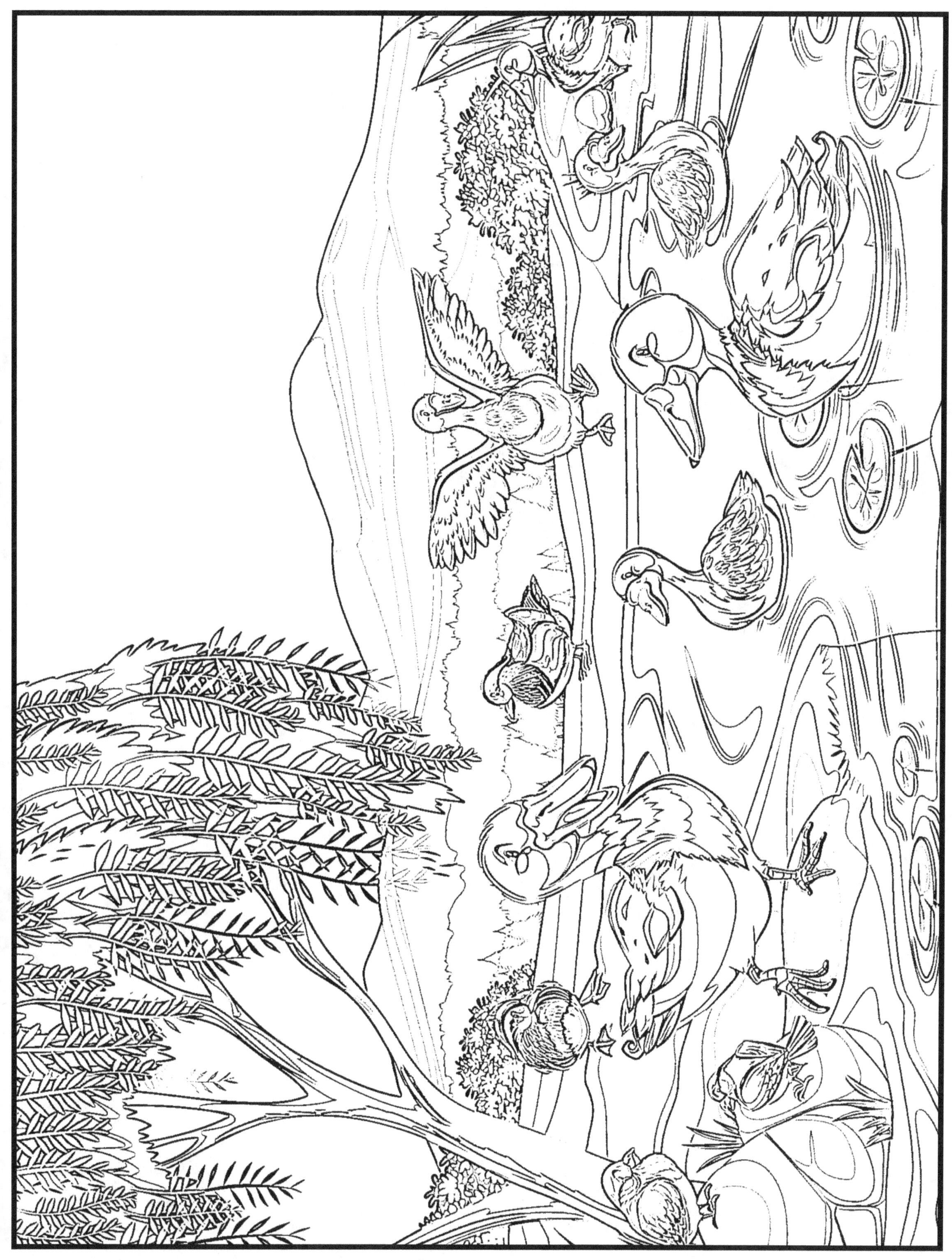